A Pictorial Guide to
WOODWORKING
PROJECTS AND TECHNIQUES

Building Unique, Beautiful, and Useful
Wood Items for Fun and Profit

JERRY SYFERT

WOODBUTCHER PRESS

A Pictorial Guide To Woodworking Projects and Techniques
Building Unique, Beautiful, and Useful Wood Items for Fun and Profit

Woodbutcher Press
ISBN-13: 978-0615648958
ISBN: 0615648959

All projects built and photographed by Jerry Syfert
Cover design and page layout by Lighthouse24

http://woodbutcherpress.com

Contents

TECHNIQUES

PROJECTS

Nothing in the world can take the place of Persistence. Talent will not; nothing is more common than unsuccessful men with talent. Genius will not; unrewarded genius is almost a proverb. Education will not; the world is full of educated derelicts. Persistence and determination alone are omnipotent. The slogan "Press On" has solved and always will solve the problems of all human kind.

Calvin Coolidge
30th president of US (1872 - 1933)

Introduction

TECHNIQUES:
Wood Art Designs, Veneering, End Grain

PROJECTS:
Lazy Susans, Cutting Boards, Wooden Banks, Boxes

As a hobbyist woodworker for over 20 years, I have developed a line of crafts that are in demand by the public. I have found that there has been very little written about the items that I present in this book. While lazy susans, cutting boards and animal banks are available by commercial manufacturers, they lack the imagination and creativity that is available to the woodworker. In this book I present basic construction methods for each item followed by more elaborate and beautiful projects. Each of these items offers the woodworker the unlimited opportunity to stretch their imagination and skills to create functional works of art. These items are fun to make, make beautiful gifts (not likely to end up in a yard sale), and are very marketable.

As an engineer, working on large main frame computers for the majority of my career, I needed a pastime that allowed me to be creative in a different way and to relieve me of my workday pressures. I started off with a radial arm saw and then gradually added to my tools as I built a cabin in the woods over a period of seven years. As my grandchildren started to join us, like many grandfathers that work with wood, I started to make wooden toys for them. They still have those toys and some of their children (my great grandchildren) are playing with them today.

My wife and I enjoyed attending the many various Arts and Craft shows that are available in the Washington DC/Baltimore, MD area where we lived. Buying tools and hardwood can become expensive although not as expensive as many other hobbies and pastimes. We decided to try our luck at exhibiting at an Arts and Craft show with our various wooden toys and try to recoup some of our costs. I could write several chapters just on our experiences while participating in the various shows (but I won't). I proceeded to build up my inventory of toys and we exhibited at our first show. It was fairly successful and we started to do more shows the following year.

I have a rather creative imagination and as our inventory and line of toys grew, so did the work and problems of transporting and exhibiting them. I found it necessary to rent a van in order to transport the toys to the shows. It took us four hours just to set up our display booth. I was working fulltime on my "Day Job" and after four years we decided to give it up. However, a year later we decided we really missed doing the shows. There is much camaraderie and friendship developed among the artists and crafters that you meet at the various shows you attend. I always envied the Jewelry Artists that showed up at a show carrying small boxes of jewelry as opposed to our vanload of toys. I came up with the idea of making unusual puzzles, which did not take up a lot of room to transport. We tried a show with them and it was quite successful. Using my methods of designing various hardwoods together, our product line grew to be very elaborate and complicated puzzles, desk clocks, lazy susans, lighthouses, cutting boards, banks, etc.

After a period of twenty years, we gave up doing the shows. I had retired from my day job and we had moved to Florida. I had always enjoyed making these items since I was unlimited in the challenge of creating various designs and utilizing my woodworking skills. I have been able to keep busy by continuing to make these items for my many friends and family and also market them in a local artists co-op.

My purpose in writing this book is to pass onto others the skills that I have developed over a twenty year period and enable them the satisfaction of being able to apply their creative talents in worthwhile projects that are of keepsake quality, make beautiful gifts and are readily marketable.

The tools I use in this book are primarily a radial arm saw, a band saw, a miter saw, a drill, a sander, a thickness planer and clamps. Whenever possible, I will suggest an alternative method or tool. You can get by without a planer if you do not resaw the boards into thinner strips but instead use boards of a standard thickness or whatever you may have on hand. Surprisingly to many, in over twenty years of woodworking, I have never owned a table saw. Many of the operations in this book can be performed more easily on a table saw than on a radial arm saw. I have nothing against table saws, it's just that I started out with a radial arm saw and have never seen the need to obtain a table saw.

The interesting part of woodworking is that there is no fixed, one way of doing a particular operation. Depending upon the skill level and tools available, given a simple project to a group of woodworkers, they would create any given project in different ways. In this book, I will show what has worked best for me, often through trial and error over a twenty five year period. You may find a better way to perform certain operations, depending upon your own tools and capabilities.

Have fun, be creative and be careful. You only get one set of eyes, lungs, ears and hands. Take care of them by using goggles, a dust mask, push sticks and ear protectors. Follow the safety guidelines published by your tool's manufacturer. Remember the Woodworkers Creed: *If it looks dangerous, it probably is.* Find an alternative method when necessary. When I first started doing woodworking I took many chances while cutting that I wouldn't even think of doing today.

This book contains two sections. The first section covers the basic construction methods, which we call *Techniques* – followed by a *Projects* section containing projects of varying difficulty. This structure provides anyone, from the novice to the more skilled woodworker, with a project of interest while allowing novices to progressively increase their skills. The projects covered include Cutting Boards, Lazy Susans, Boxes, and Animal Shaped Banks. However, once the basic construction methods outlined in the first section are mastered, the woodworker may apply those techniques to many projects other than those presented in this book.

1

Wood Laminating Design Techniques
The Stair Step Design

In **this section** we will be learning how to create wood art by gluing together different hardwoods to create various patterns. This will allow a person to create wood material in which they will then be able to make beautiful items that will allow them to apply their creativity, talents and imagination.

I have read books that presented this concept in such a format that a person would need to be an engineer or have a major in trigonometry in order to understand it. This section (Chapters 1–6) is devoted entirely to the creation of various wood designs and *easy* methods of creating them. The second section (Chapters 7–15) is devoted to using these wood designs in various projects.

We will start out with an easy to create design that is very attractive although you won't think so as we start this design. This is about as easy as it gets, starting by gluing two boards together (can't get much easier than that).

Cut a piece of walnut and a piece of maple (or oak), 24" long and both 3" wide which after edge gluing gives you a board 6" wide. You could also use any two contrasting woods. These are a little over 3/4" thick but the thickness is not really relevant in this operation. Next, edge glue the two pieces together. I prefer to put a piece of wax paper over newspapers when gluing. The newspaper prevents glue-up on your work surface and the wax paper prevents your project from becoming glued to the newspaper. I prefer to use yellow carpenters glue for my projects and having tried many different brands, I fail to find any difference in the results. I buy my glue by the gallon and have found that a used mustard bottle serves very well as a dispenser. So far, couldn't be easier but it doesn't sound very attractive. Hang in there.

Photo 1-1: Edge glue and then clamp the two boards together

For practice, if you want and you don't have any contrasting hardwoods, use two pieces of a pine board and stain one piece the color of walnut. This will give you an inexpensive way to try this out. My experience has been that you put a lot of time and effort into a project, the cost of the wood may be your least consideration. Particularly when you make veneers out of your glue up, the cost per project drops way down, regardless of which hardwoods you use.

After the glue has done its job (I usually let mine set for four hours or overnight), the next step is to cut pieces at an angle from the board. I will use my miter saw but they could be cut just as easily using a table saw or a radial arm saw. The reason I made the board 6" wide was so I would be able to make the cuts using the miter saw which has a 12" blade. The other consideration is that if your glue up exceeds six inches, you may not be able to cut it into veneers unless you have a band saw that can cut wood thicker than six inches. Because these two pieces ended up being 6" wide, the largest angle I could cut was 30 deg. with the miter saw. If you are using a table saw, cut it at a 45 deg. The angle is not critical. Using the miter saw, start by cutting the corner off.

Photo 1-2: Cutting off the end of the board

Photo 1-3: Cutting off a 5/8" piece

I next place a stop block on the saw so I can make cuts 5/8" wide. I then cut off ten pieces, 5/8" wide.

These pieces are not glued together and are just placed into position to form a design. They are flat across the top, they only look like stair steps.

By flipping every other piece, end for end you get a design with a 3D appearance. These pieces are perfectly flat across the top. If you decide to go with this design, instead of the next step, cut off five more of the 5/8" pieces.

Going back to the miter saw, reset the stop block so that it will be making cuts of 1/4" wide, then cut 12 pieces.

By realigning the pieces back to the first configuration we had as shown in Photo 1-4, we can now place the 1/4" wide pieces in between the 5/8" wide pieces but with the walnut pieces

Photo 1-4: Pieces flipped and turned, a really EASY stair step design to make

Photo 1-5: Making 1/4" cuts

Photo 1-6: Placing the 5/8" pieces and 1/4" pieces together.

reversed so they are next to the maple. This will result in a striking design which appears to be two sets of stairs. There again, they are perfectly flat on top, although they appear to be three dimensional. These pieces have not been glued together yet at this stage.

The next step is to carefully glue the pieces together while keeping them in alignment.

Apply the glue to the edge of a piece and spread the glue using a glue brush. Be sure and cover the entire area, do not leave any dry spots. You may use your finger but that tends to get pretty messy when you are gluing a lot of pieces.

Before you start to glue the pieces together, carefully check that each piece is in its proper position. It is very easy to misalign the pieces. While gluing one piece at a time, it's easy to turn the piece in your hand and then gluing it into the wrong position. Check each piece before you attach it. Nothing like spending hours on a project and then realize you glued a piece in wrong. Been there, done that. After applying the glue,

Photo 1-7: Gluing the pieces using a glue brush

slide the piece back and forth across the new piece to spread the glue. While gluing a lot of pieces together, as in this procedure, I prefer to clamp them together after gluing only half of them. This allows you to clamp them together before the glue becomes too dry. Use a clamp in the center and gently tighten it, being careful to not knock the pieces out of alignment. Do not over tighten at this time as you may cause the pieces to slip their alignment. Place a clamp at each end and tighten. Now go back and further tighten the clamps. When done, you should have two sets of glued pieces and after drying you can then glue them into one piece. However, as you go through the project section of this book you will find projects that do not require a piece of wood that large and may prefer to leave them as two separate glued up wood designs.

Photo 1-8: Gluing half of
the strips together

Photo 1-9: Gluing the two sections
into one piece

Cutting Off The Ends

Rough sand the glue up to make the surface flat, prior to cutting the ends off, 60 grit sandpaper in a hand oscillating sander works good for this.

If you went with the first design as shown in *Photo 1-4*, you can cut off the ends at a right angle. However the nature of the beast of the second design puts the pieces together leaving an angle on the ends. This requires you to find the proper angle to cut off the ends.

Photo 1-10: Cutting off the ends

Using a straight edge, draw a line across the edge of the end pieces to establish the cutting line. Since I am using a radial arm saw, I raised the blade to be above the cutting line and adjusted the angle to coincide with the line. I then locked the angle in place, lowered the blade and made the cut. I then flipped the glued up piece and cut the ends off the other end at the exact same angle.

Photo 1-11: Finished glued up block

Wood Laminating Design Techniques
Fancy Stair Step Design

This is a version of the first design, using a different wood combination and is very easy to create – it only looks difficult.

In this design I have used a combination of walnut and maple on the outside edges, the same as the first design but have inserted zebrawood and padauk into the center to present a familiar but different look. Padauk, purpleheart, zebrawood and some other exotic hardwoods tend to be oily and therefore do not always glue well. I have found that wiping the gluing surface of these woods first with lacquer thinner and letting dry prior to gluing works very well to alleviate this problem. If you do not have lacquer thinner on hand, you might try paint thinner instead. Padauk is very toxic, I strongly recommend that you wear a dust mask when cutting this type of wood. You should always wear a dust mask when working with wood, but especially with padauk.

I used pieces 20" long. The walnut and maple are both 1-3/4" wide, the zebrawood is 1" wide and the padauk is 3/4" wide. A piece of maple instead of the red padauk would also make a very nice combination. The combination came out to be 6-1/2" wide.

You may use any combination of wood for this design.

Photo 2-1: Pieces being cut to 5/8" wide.

This beautiful design is really very simple to make and by using various wood combination there is practically no limit as to what design you may create.

I cut the pieces at 30 deg and 5/8" wide (as shown in *Photo 2-1*). I ended up with 17 pieces. Use a hand held, folded piece of sandpaper to remove the "fuzzy" edges from the bottom of the cuts. This gives you the following combinations to choose from to glue together.

Photo 2-2: Aligning the ends gives you this design

Photo 2-3: Flipping every other piece, end to end, creates this design

By turning and flipping from end to end, every other piece, you will have the second design. This is the design I will glue together in the manner previously described. One advantage of this design over some of the previous designs is that the ends may be cut off at a right angle rather than trying to find the correct slanted angle to cut the end pieces off.

Photo 2-4: Finished piece with ends cut off

In the Projects section, you will find projects that can use thicker pieces of glue ups and other projects where thinner pieces may be used. It is sometimes a waste to use a thicker piece of your glue up that you have spent a lot of time, effort and material cost when you can resaw your glue ups into thinner pieces and use as a veneer. We will see how to do this at the end of this section.

3

Wood Laminating Design Techniques
The Checkerboard Design

Cut four pieces of walnut and four pieces of oak or other contrasting woods. Cut the pieces 22" x 1" x 1". The thickness need not be 1" but we will be using this piece in the Project Section and will want the board to be 1" thick. If you want to use the checkerboard design for another purpose you may make it whatever thickness you want. Glue the eight pieces together, alternating the wood. Use a glue brush, wax paper and clamps as before.

Photo 3-1: Checkerboard Design

Photo 3-2: Clamping the strips together

Photo 3-3: Measuring the exact width of the boards

Photo 3-4: Set the stop block to 5/8" to cut the pieces

When cutting off the pieces it is necessary to get the width as close as possible to the width of the oak and walnut pieces that you are using. Prior to gluing the pieces together, cut off a small piece to be used as a "width gauge." You can also measure the width of a piece and set up the stop block accordingly but it is more accurate to use a block of wood as a gauge. With this setup I was able to cut nineteen pieces to be used for the glue up.

By shifting the cut pieces a half square over you will get one design. By flipping every other piece end for end, you will get a checkerboard design.

Photo 3-5: A design by simply shifting the pieces

Photo 3-6: Flipping over every other piece to create a checkerboard design

I glued up eleven pieces into one block and eight pieces into a second block. This will provide two different size blocks to be used in the project section.

Photo 3-7: Eleven piece block

Photo 3-8: Two blocks glued up

4

Wood Laminating Design Techniques
The Deluxe Herringbone Design

Cut four pieces of walnut and four pieces of oak or other contrasting woods, same as in the checkerboard design. Cut the pieces 24" x 1" out of 3/4" thick standard stock. If you are cutting these out of rough cut lumber and then planeing, the dimensions only need to be approximate but try to stay close to the 3/4" size.

Glue the eight pieces together, alternating the wood types with the glue on the 1" side surface and the 3/4" width on the top surface. Use a glue brush and wax paper. You can do this using 6" clamps. You will notice in the picture that I staggered the boards on the ends. The only purpose of this is to waste a little less lumber as the initial cut is to cut off the ends at an angle and it is wasted. Don't be concerned about the glue beading up as you tighten the clamps, this will be either planed or sanded off.

After drying, if you have a planer, plane both surfaces smooth, if not, use 60 grit sandpaper to smooth the surface and remove the glue. The next steps will be similar to the first lamination. Since this piece ended up being 5-1/2" wide, I was able to set the angle at 45deg. If your piece is wider and you are using a miter saw, back off on the angle to something less until the blade will reach to cut all the way through the width of the glued up board.

Photo 4-1: Clamping the strips together

The next step is the same as in the first two laminations, set up a fence to make 5/8" wide cuts at 45 deg. and cut *eleven* pieces.

Photo 4-2: Cutting the end at 45 degrees

Photo 4-3: Cutting the 5/8" pieces

This will enable you to make the following configurations by flipping and turning the various pieces.

Photo 4-4: Design by aligning the ends

Starting with the original configuration (*Photo 4-4,* left), flip every other piece, end for end, without turning a piece over. This will result in this very attractive, different and easy design to make. This design also allows you to cut the ends off at right angles.

Photo 4-5: Design by turning over every other piece

Photo 4-6: A third configuration by simply realigning the pieces

If you wish to stick with this design do not go on to the next step of cutting pieces of 1/4" width (same as in the first lamination design) but instead cut out five more pieces of the 5/8" width that you have your saw already set up for and use this attractive design.

However, since this is a "how to" book I will take this design one step further. As in the first design, set your saw to cut out ¼" width pieces and cut eleven pieces.

Photo 4-7: Cut pieces 1/4" wide

Photo 4-8: A simple configuration

With the pieces again assembled as in the original configuration (above right), insert the 1/4" pieces in between every other 5/8" piece with opposite opposing colors. Next glue the pieces together in two separate blocks using six inch clamps. Follow the guidelines presented in the first glue up, that is, use wax paper and a glue brush. Start by tightening the center clamp first but do not over tighten being careful to maintain the design alignment, then apply the two end clamps and tighten all three.

Photo 4-9: Inserting the 5/8"
and 1/4" pieces together

Photo 4-10: Clamping half of
the pieces together

As before, clamp the two sections together, rough sand the surfaces, mark and cut off the end pieces as instructed in the first glue up.

Photo 4-11: A beautiful, unusual and attractive design

Wood Laminating Design Techniques
Creating Design Veneers

Many of the projects in this book do not require the use of a thick piece of material such as the ones we just glued up. A cutting board is one area where you would want to use a thick piece as opposed to using a veneer cut from the glued up block. One of the limitations I personally have is that my band saw will not cut material over six inches thick. If you can cut a piece thicker than six inches you may resaw some of the pieces we just glued up. This is not that big a problem as you may use more that one veneer in a project. For example, the lazy susan shown here was constructed by using two veneer pieces cut from the same glue up. This method will be shown in the *Projects* section in the Lazy Susans chapter.

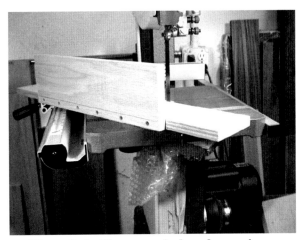

Photo 5-1: *Homemade band saw fence*

When resawing lumber into veneers, I prefer to use a higher fence than the one that normally comes with a saw. I screwed two pieces of oak veneer plywood together at right angles. It could be made of any scrap lumber as long as the lumber is not warped. The pieces are 4-1/2 " wide and the shorter piece which acts as the fence, is 16" long. The longer piece is 26" long and is used to clamp the fence to the saw table.

It is important before you start cutting your veneers to check and make sure your saw table is at a right angle with the saw blade. I use a 1/2 inch blade for resawing the veneers. I am sure that you as well as I, have read many articles about resawing and setting your fence at an angle to correspond with the blade drift and having pivot points to allow you to move the work piece to follow a line. Well, I don't do any of this and have been very successful in over twenty years of cutting veneers.

Photo 5-2: *Checking the blade to be at a right angle with the table*

Photo 5-3: *Resawing a veneer from a block*

I set my 4-1/2" fence parallel with the blade at the proper distance for the width of the veneer piece. I then hold the piece up tight against the fence while using a push stick to advance the piece through the blade. By putting the piece the width you want the veneer to be against the fence (back of the blade), it then allows you to make more veneers the *same* thickness without having to move the fence.

Photo 5-4: Three veneers cut to the same thickness

If you set the fence so your desired piece is *away* from the fence (this side of the blade), you will then have to move the fence for further cuts and the resulting pieces will not be of the same thickness. This is in addition to the hassle of having to relocate the fence each time. This is NOT the way to do it.

Photo 5-5: Cutting the veneer with the desired piece away from the fence

Photo 5-6: Three pieces cut to different thickness

Photo 5-7: Veneers cut to various thicknesses

I have cut veneers less than 1/16" using this method.

All of the lazy Susans and desk clocks that I make use veneers. By utilizing veneers, a glued up design can go a long way.

Photo 5-8: Clocks made from design veneers

Wood Laminating Design Techniques
Veneering

This chapter is about an *easy* way to use beautiful veneer to create unusual and attractive items. This method is not in concourse with traditional veneering methods. If you have ever done any serious, complicated veneering, you will know what I mean. Having said this, I will show you how to do it the easy way, which works well for the lazy susans and other items shown in the *Projects* Section.

You will not need any special tools such as veneer saws, banding material, special knives, vacuum pump, special glue, veneer tape, electric iron, steaming equipment, etc. If you are experienced in working with veneer or have read any books on veneering, you are shaking your head, about to have a heart attack, and about now saying "no way!!!" The reason I can say this is quite easy, it's because the projects we will be making are just that, "quite *easy*." Straight, flat work, using single pieces of veneer without veneer joints.

If, after doing some of the simple veneering as shown in this chapter you have the desire to do some *real* veneering, I suggest you purchase one of several books available on the subject. You will find it is a different ball game altogether. True veneering is an art unto itself and is a skill you will not master overnight nor here.

Unless you have a place within your vicinity where you can purchase veneers, you will have to do as I do and purchase it online. Do *not* do a search for just *veneer* as you will bring up sites for *dental veneers*. Search for *wood veneer* and you will be in woodworker's heaven. You will find that these beautiful veneers such as burls can be quite expensive. However, if you were to use solid lumber made from a burl you would find it *really* costly, especially in the size needed for some of the projects we will be constructing. If you go to eBay and search for wood veneer, it will bring up many sites where you may then search for exactly the size and type of veneers you are interested in.

I normally make my lazy susans 16" in diameter. Therefore I never buy veneers less then 16" wide. I do not use backed veneers as it is not necessary for this type of veneering and more expensive than non-backed. If you make a 16" diameter lazy susan and the piece of veneer you are using is larger, you may always use the unused sections for smaller projects such as banks, clocks, pencil boxes, etc. Many burl type veneers may have small holes in them. For our purpose they may easily be filled with wood putty.

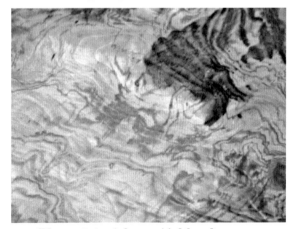

Photo 6-1: A beautiful burl veneer

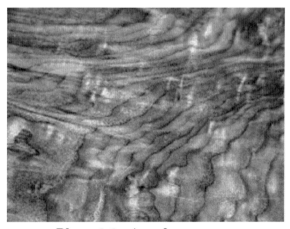

Photo 6-2: A walnut veneer

If you are using burls and even most other straight grain veneers, you will find that they do not lie flat but instead are quite curly because of the nature of the grain structure within the burl itself and the way that veneer is cut from the log.

When the burl is cut to its nominal thin dimension of around 1/32 of an inch (some are slightly thinner and others slightly thicker) it tends to become curly and wavy. It is necessary to flatten the pieces. This is done by compressing the veneer between two pieces of MDF (Medium Density Fiberboard) which has a laminated surface. The two pieces I use are 18" square and were cut from a larger piece. If you wish to limit your lazy susans or any other project to less than 16", then you may purchase shelving which is available in 16" widths.

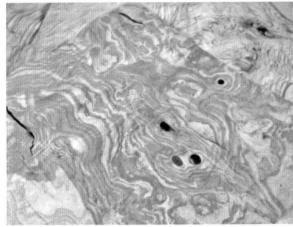

Photo 6-3: Another burl veneer

Photo 6-4: MDF boards used to flatten the veneers

Obviously we need something to glue the veneer to. It's known as a substrate. I prefer to use ½" thick MDF board for most projects of this type and occasionally 1/4" thick. While it is available in 4'x 8' sheets, I prefer to buy it in 2'x 4' pieces because of the weight and ease of handling while cutting to size. For a 16" lazy susan I will cut the pieces to 18" square. The 6" pieces left over may be saved and used in smaller projects.

Photo 6-5: MDF 1/2" boards used to glue the veneer to

Photo 6-6: *Boards that will be used to clamp the center of the veneers flat*

Cut two pieces of scrap 2x4's to 18" long. Glue a small piece of scrap veneer to the center of the edges of the 2x4's. Set these aside until later when we will use them to clamp the center of the 18" square veneer piece to the substrate.

After selecting a piece of veneer, it must first be made pliable, cut to size and then glued to a substrate of 1/2" MDF. You cannot cut the veneer while it is dry and brittle. You must exercise a certain amount of care in handling while dry to prevent it from splitting.

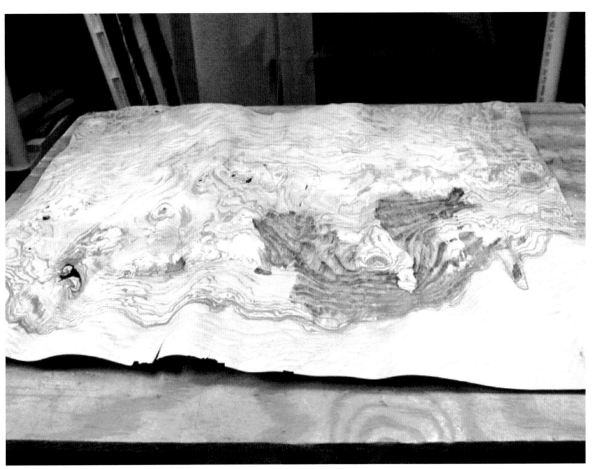

Photo 6-7: *Select a piece of veneer to be used for this project.
It will need to be flattened*

An inexpensive misting bottle is available from various stores and used to wet the surface of both sides of the veneer. Although most books on veneering recommend the addition of alcohol and other substances, for our purpose in doing easy, flat veneering, plain old tap water works fine.

Photo 6-8: Use a spray bottle to dampen the veneer

Photo 6-9: Spray the water on both sides of the veneer

Spray both sides until it is thoroughly wet. It will then become quite pliable and easier to handle.

Next we will place the 18" square of laminated MDF board over the top of the wet veneer. Using the edge of the MDF board as a straight edge guideline, we will cut the veneer to an 18" square. Since we are not

Photo 6-10: After spraying with water, the veneer is now flexible

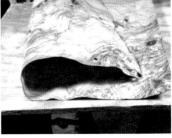

Photo 6-11: Since the veneer is now flexible you will be able to press it flat

concerned about obtaining a super straight cut for joining purposes, a utility knife will work fine. I recommend however, that you start with a fresh sharp blade. Since we will be using this piece in the Project Section to make a beautiful lazy susan, all edges will be removed when it is cut into a circle.

Photo 6-12: Place the board over the veneer

Photo 6-13: Use the board as a straight edge while trimming to size

Apply and spread glue over the surface of the MDF substrate. I buy my yellow carpenter's glue by the gallon and use a mustard bottle as a glue dispenser.

Photo 6-14: Apply glue to the surface of the 18" x 18" piece of MDF

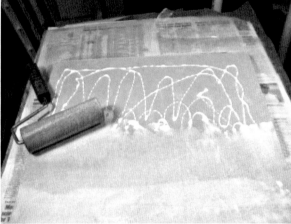

Photo 6-15: Spread the glue evenly over the surface of the board

Place wax paper over the veneer. This is important to prevent glue that may ooze through tiny holes in the veneer onto the clamping pieces.

Photo 6-16: Place the veneer on the board

Photo 6-17: Place wax paper over the veneer

Place a piece of the clamping MDF underneath the assembly and another one on the top.

Place a clamp approximately every 3" around the outside edges. If you do not have a lot of clamps, you may place them further apart. Now is when you want to use the two 2 x 4's that you previously had glued a small piece of veneer into the center. Clamp the two pieces so they will apply pressure upon the center of the board.

Photo 6-18: Make a sandwich of the glued up pieces

Photo 6-19: Place a clamp every 3" on the assembly and use the 2x4 board clamps

Depending upon the piece of veneer, there may be small holes and minute cracks that appear. This hole is less than 1/8" in diameter. These holes and cracks may easily be filled with wood putty and then sanded over.

You must be very careful when sanding veneer, I never use anything coarser than 220 grit sand paper.

Photo 6-20: The veneer is now firmly attached to the 18" substrate

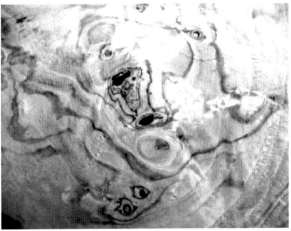

Photo 6-21: You may have small holes in the veneer

You may also have small cracks appear in the veneer. These too may be easily filled with wood putty and sanded flat.

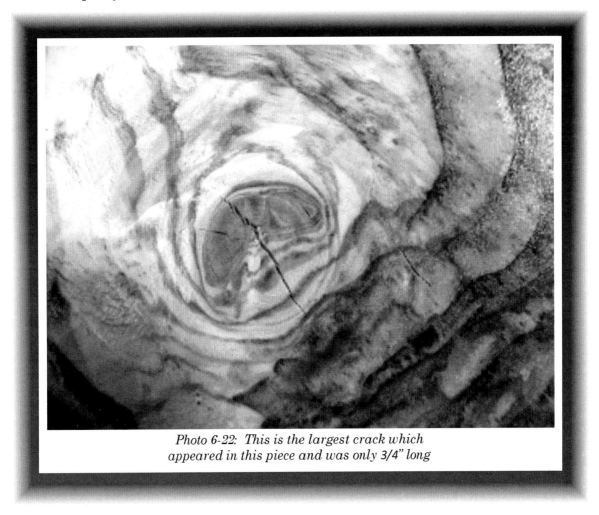

Photo 6-22: This is the largest crack which appeared in this piece and was only 3/4" long

We will use this piece in the *Projects* Section to create a lazy susan.

7

Wood Laminating Design Techniques
Creating End Grain

In this chapter you will learn how to use inexpensive Southern Pine construction lumber to create very attractive projects. In the *Projects* section is where we will use this lumber to create various projects. This chapter will deal only in the creation of the end grain material.

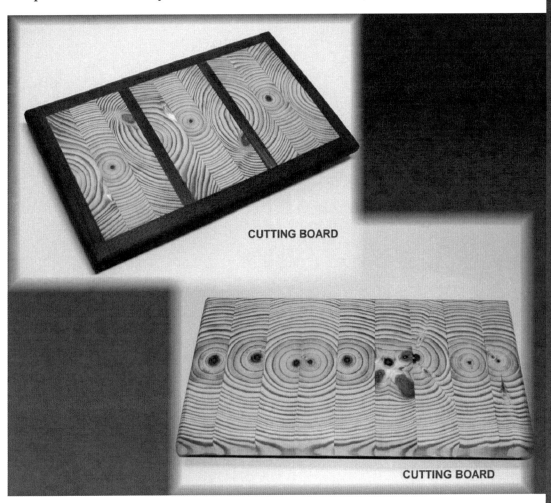

CUTTING BOARD

CUTTING BOARD

We will start with the purchase of a 2"x 8", 8' piece of lumber from our local lumber yard or box store. When purchasing the lumber, pay close attention to the end grain of the board. You may or may not want knots to show. Knots will inevitably show up eventually as you proceed through the cutting of the boards but they will probably be much smaller than knots that you will see at the end of the board you are purchasing. Try to purchase a board that is flat and not cupped as you will be cutting and gluing the board back together. Do not buy wet lumber.

Photo 7-1: Southern Pine construction lumber

The next step will be to cut the board into four equal pieces approximately two feet long.

Set aside one piece for now. You could have cut the board into three pieces but they would have been 32" long and difficult to work with.

Even though you may have purchased a board that appears very flat, chances are that you may find it may not be perfectly flat when you go to glue the three pieces together.

If you have a surface planer, you should plane the surfaces of the three pieces so that they fit together without a gap. If your board is reasonably flat to start with, you shouldn't have to do much planing.

As in the other glue up projects, you will be able to change the design by shifting the pieces around. Shown here are different designs by rearranging the three pieces.

Photo 7-2: Different configurations by simply rearranging the lumber pieces

Using yellow carpenters glue, spread the glue over one of the boards. I have found that a 6" rubber wallpaper roller is an excellent way to spread the glue rapidly and evenly. It is also very easy to clean.

Photo 7-3: Apply the glue generously   *Photo 7-4: Spreading the glue using a roller*

Glue the three pieces together and clamp them approximately every three inches.

You will find that no matter how careful you are in gluing the three boards together, the edges of the boards will probably be uneven. Along with the rounded edges of the boards, you will be prevented from having an even edge. It is not a problem.

Photo 7-5: Clamp the three boards together every 3 inches   *Photo 7-6: Check to see that the boards are even*

Photo 7-7: Smoothing the edges with a jointer

If you have a jointer, plane the edges of the board until smooth. If not, simply wait until after you have sliced the pieces off of the block and then cut off the ends.

The block is two feet long and weighs fifteen pounds. Since we will be working at cutting the ends off, it is difficult to work with at that size. Therefore, cut it in half using the band saw with a 1/2", 3-TPI (Teeth Per Inch) blade. You can also use a table saw if it will cut 4.5"thick lumber.

Photo 7-8:
Cutting the board
in half with a band saw

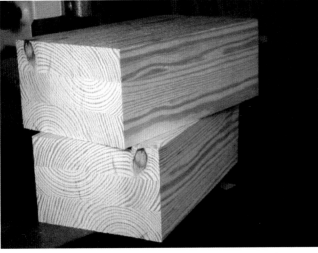

Photo 7-9:
The two blocks of
wood after cutting in half

This will give you two blocks that are one foot long and weigh 7.5 lbs and are much easier to control and handle. Next we will be cutting pieces from the end of the block.

If you have a table saw that will cut 4.5" thick lumber, you will get a smoother cut than using a 1/2", 3-TPI band saw blade. Check to ensure that your blade is square with your saw table. If it isn't, adjust according to your saw's manual.

I cut eight pieces, 1/4" thick and six pieces, 1-1/4" thick. These will be used in the project section to make pencil boxes or other projects and the thicker pieces will be used primarily for making Cutting Boards.

Photo 7-10:
Check to ensure
the blade is
square with
the table

Photo 7-11:
Cutting a 1/4"
slice from the
block of wood

At this point you still have another one foot block of wood for future projects. You also have a single, two foot board that we did not use. This is a very economical way to create beautiful project lumber at practically no cost and easy to do.

Photo 7-12: Blocks of wood after cutting, to be used in projects

Photo 7-13: Pencil box with clock and desk clock

8

Wood Laminated Design Projects
Lazy Susan, Veneered

The term *Lazy Susan* first came into use around 1917 and was used to describe a revolving server. It may be constructed of just about any material. While most commercially marketed lazy susans are made of solid materials such as wood, plastic, marble and glass, the purpose of this book is to show how to construct them by gluing together various hardwoods into beautiful but still functional works of art.

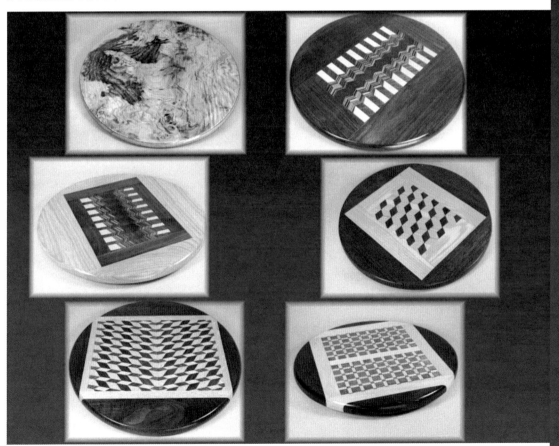

Photo 8-1: Lazy susans make excellent wedding gifts

While most commercially purchased lazy susans are probably used on kitchen tables, I have found that most of the ones that I have created end up on coffee tables as well as kitchen tables, as a work of art. Once the basic steps of construction are learned and mastered, a person is limited only by their own creativity, imagination and talent.

In this chapter we will discuss lazy susan basics, construct a simple basic lazy susan followed by more complicated but still *easy* designs.

The basic construction of a lazy susan consists of a flat base, square or round (most are square), which revolves on roller bearings.

The type shown in *Photo 8-2* is the most common and readily available at your local hardware stores, woodworking catalogs and online through the internet. This square type comes in various sizes but for the 16" diameter lazy susans described in this book, the 6" will work the best and will support a load of 500 lbs. If you go to the trouble and expense of making an elaborate and beautiful lazy susan, it doesn't make much sense to cover it up with a TV or any other large, heavy object. The most common use is on a kitchen table, buffet or coffee table with small items that do not cover the lazy susan's beautiful craftsmanship (and your hard work).

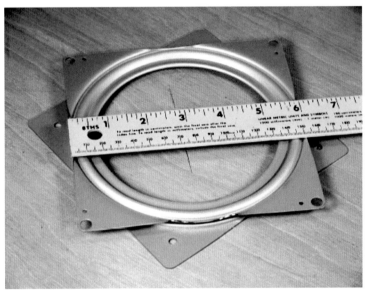

Photo 8-2: 6" square bearings

We will start by making a 16" diameter lazy susan. You may make yours larger or smaller if you like. I found that the 16" is like Goldilocks and the three bears, not too big and not too small but rather just right. I will be making this first one using the veneered board which was made in the Techniques Section. You may elect to first make any of the lazy susans shown since basic construction is the same with the difference being in the design of the top.

If you want, you may simply glue some boards together to form a square larger than 16". The board I will be using is the 18" veneered board made in Chapter 6 ("Veneering").

The first step will be to find the center of the board by turning it over so the backside is up. Draw a line from corner to corner on the backside to form an X. Drill a small hole in the center of the board, being careful to not go all of the way through the board. Place a small screw into the hole, attach a pencil to a piece of string, cord or fish line and draw a 16" diameter circle. Next, using a band saw, cut out the circle. This is fairly straight forward and easy to do.

Photo 8-3: Previously constructed 18"x 18" veneered MDF board 1/2" thick

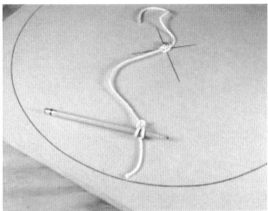

Photo 8-4: Draw a 16" diameter circle using a string and pencil with a screw located in the center

Using a rounding over router bit, size of your choice with a ball bearing guide, place the veneer side down and route the edge. Make sure you are going against the cutting surface. Routers turn the cutter counter clockwise so feed the lazy susan CCW as well.

Fill any cracks or voids you may have with wood putty. Depending upon the veneer you are using, you may have many or none. The next step is sanding the surface and the rounded over edges. Veneer is very thin and care must be used in sanding. If you use an orbital sander and 220 grit sandpaper you should have no problem obtaining a smooth surface without going through the veneer. I never sand veneer with anything coarser than 220 grit sandpaper.

Photo 8-5: Route the top edge of the lazy susan with a rounding over bit

I use a 50/50 combination of linseed oil and paint thinner to apply to all of my wood projects. I keep a coffee can containing this mixture with a lid on it. This will enhance the grain of any project and still accept most any finish. Apply sparingly with a rag and do not flood the surface as you normally would.

Veneer is very porous and if you apply too much oil it can soak through and loosen the glue and buckle the veneer (voice of experience). The next step is to apply a finish of your choice. I prefer to use water base polyurethane. It is easy to apply and has very little odor. Start by coating the bottom with whatever finish you are using. You must coat the bottom of the lazy susans as well as the top to prevent warping.

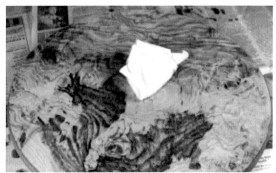

Photo 8-6: Wipe a coat of linseed oil and paint thinner combination sparingly to highlight the grain in the veneer

Creating a Base

The top is done and now we need to create a base. The six inch bearings require a board made 7-1/4" square. If you make the board wider than 7-1/4" wide, you will not be able to screw the base to the top. It can be made of any material as it does not show after being installed. The thickness is not important and can also be made of standard 3/4" stock. However it should be at least ½" thick in order to accommodate a 1/2" long screw.

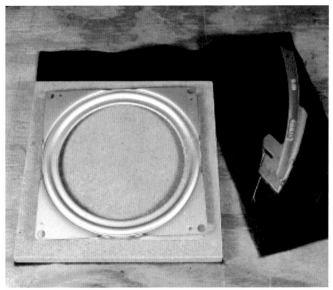

Photo 8-7: Place the base upon the felt and cut along the edges

I will be using 1/2" thick MDF board along with some thin washers. We do not want to have bare wood on the bottom of the base as it could scratch the surface upon which it is resting. You could simply place felt sticky pads on the bottom but I prefer to glue a piece of felt on the bottom. Felt is available from any craft store and can be glued onto the base using wood glue or use the self sticking kind. An easy way to cut the felt to size is to place the base on top of the felt and use a cutter along the edges prior to mounting to the top.

Center the bearings upon the base board with the small holes upon the board. Mark the holes for drilling holes for the mounting screws. Use #8, 1/2" long screws.

All 1/2" screws are not necessarily the same length so it's a good idea to use small washers with the screws. Drill small holes in the board and screw the bearings to the base.

Photo 8-8: Center the bearings upon the base and mark the small holes

Photo 8-9: Center the bearings and mark the holes for drilling

Place the bearings upon the bottom of the lazy susan and center it. With a 16" diameter top the edges of the bearings will be approximately 4" from the edges of the top piece. Mark the large holes and drill small holes in the top, being very careful to not penetrate the top all of the way through. Mount the board to the top in the same manner as attaching the base using #8, 1/2" screws and washers.

Spread glue evenly on the base and attach the previously cut felt to the base.

Photo 8-10: Apply glue to the base and apply the felt

You have now completed a basic lazy susan and by following these guide lines you will be able to create a variety of attractive lazy susans. Next we will construct a lazy susan using art design glue ups.

Photo 8-11: Finished Lazy Susan

9

Wood Laminated Design Projects
Lazy Susan, Wood Design

We will start by selecting a design block as made in the *Techniques* section on Wood Laminated Designs. I will use this one which I have made 3/4" thick which is the same thickness of standard lumber. You may use any type of wood for the edges, I will be using walnut but maple also looks very nice with this particular design.

Since I normally make 16" diameter lazy susans, I have made a 16" blank out of paneling to use as a gauge. This could also be made of cardboard or whatever. Your design will quite possibly be of a different size. By placing it upon a blank, you will be able to measure what size boards you will need to use for the edges. The board widths should be a *minimum* of a 1/2" wider than the measurement shown, in this case 5" and 3-3/4" wide. You could just use 5" wide stock or wider.

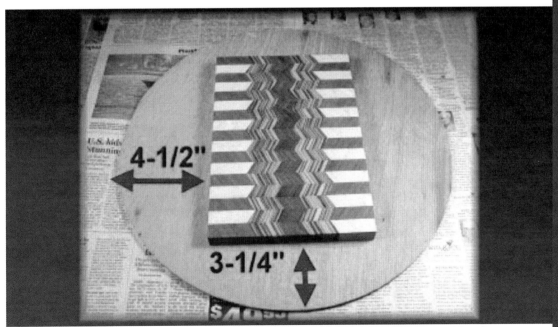

Photo 9-1: Place the glued up design upon a 16" diameter blank

Your measurements will be different, depending upon the size of your glue up. In this case the lengths of the longer boards are 17" and the shorter boards are cut to a length to be a 1/2 inch longer than the width. These will be cut off evenly after gluing. See *Photo 9-2*.

Photo 9-2: Size of the boards being used to create a minimum of a 17" square to cut out a 16" diameter lazy susan

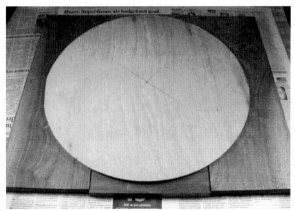

Photo 9-3: Checking the board size with a 16" blank

After I determine the size of the boards being used, I like to place the blank upon the boards as a double check on the size. If you come up a little short, just make your lazy susan a smaller diameter.

Place wax paper on your workbench and edge glue the two shorter pieces to the glue up using two bar clamps.

Photo 9-4: Edge glue the two shorter pieces to the ends of the design glue up

The next step will be removing the protruding ends of the short boards. This can be done using a table saw or a radial arm saw. Cut slightly into the glue up to ensure a smooth surface for the two longer boards to be glued.

If you are using Bessey type bar clamps, place wax paper over the bars and then edge glue and clamp the two longer pieces to the glue up sides.

Photo 9-5: Cut the edges of the board to be smooth and even

Photo 9-6: Edge glue and clamp the two side pieces to the glue up

After drying overnight, it will be necessary to locate the center of the *design* block. On the *bottom*, draw an "X" in the center of the *design* by measuring from corner to corner of the *design (NOT the entire piece)*. If you measure from the corners of the walnut, you probably won't end up in the center of the glue up.

Using an 11/64" drill bit, drill a hole in the "X" location, being very careful to not go all of the way through and end up with a hole in the top surface of the lazy susan. You can prevent this by marking the drill bit with tape to limit the depth of the hole so as not to go too deep.

Photo 9-7: Drill the center hole in the glue up

After drilling the hole you may draw a circle of 16" diameter using the pencil/string method as previously described in *Photo 8-4*.

Photo 9-8:
Cut out the circle using either a circle jig or the pencil/string method to mark the circle

Using the router as shown in *Photo 9-8* and creating a base as shown in the previous chapter, finish up the lazy susan.

Photo 9-9: Finished Lazy Susan

10

Wood Laminated Design Projects
Lazy Susan, Using a Laminated Design Glue Up Veneer

To maximize the effort and expensive wood that is put into creating a glue up, we will use veneers cut from the design glue ups as shown in Chapter 5. This will give you an opportunity to become creative in making various configurations. Instead of making one lazy susan as in the last creation you can make two different ones using one glued up design. As seen in the following photos, it is easy to reposition the sliced veneers into different positions. I will start by using the previously mentioned 16" blank made of either wood or cardboard to use as a template for sizing the lazy susan.

Here we are only positioning pieces to see how they would come together to make a 16" diameter lazy susan. This was configured using sliced veneer glue ups made in Chapter 5. The veneers will be glued to 1/2" MDF board to provide an adequate thickness.

Photo 10-1: Laying out the wood pieces to check for size

Photo 10-2: Another layout

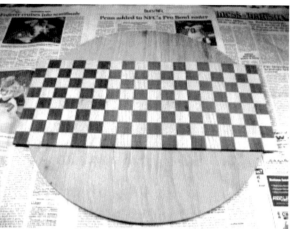

Photo 10-3: Another layout

Photo 10-4: A layout after gluing to 1/2" MDF

Photo 10-5: Completed lazy susan after being trimmed out with maple and walnut

All of the above configurations may be trimmed out using woods of your choice. The checkerboard design in *Photo 10-3* would most likely look best if trimmed out using oak and walnut since that is what the design is made of. The design in *Photos 10-1* and *10-2* would be best trimmed in maple or padauk or walnut. The design in *Photo 10-5* was trimmed in maple and walnut, even though there was no walnut in the design. Let your imagination run wild but try to maintain good taste in your creation. You're the boss, satisfy yourself and bring forth your inner creativity. Most of all, have fun.

I have selected the design that follows as constructed in Chapter 4. I sliced the design into three veneers as previously shown. I will be using only two of the slices in this project in which we will be attaching them to 1/2" MDF board.

Before starting the assembly I placed the pieces upon a scrap piece of MDF to raise them to the proper height and then placed them upon my 16" diameter template to check for size and the placement of oak pieces to trim it out. The vacant edges will be filled with walnut. Since the lamination itself is comprised of oak and walnut, this will make a good combination to finish it out.

Photo 10-6: Place the parts upon the template to check for size and appearance

The easiest way to do this would be to just trim the design with walnut. However since this is a "how to" book, I will take it a step further and trim it first with oak and then walnut.

Cut a piece of 1/2" MDF to the size of the two pieces of design. Glue them to the MDF. Be careful when clamping that the pieces do not slip out of alignment with each other. Line up at least one edge even with edge of the MDF. This is so you will have a straight edge to trim the block.

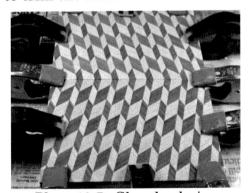

Photo 10-7: Glue the design slices to the 1/2" MDF board

Photo 10-8: Clamp the end pieces to the glued up design

After drying, trim the edges to be perfectly flush with the MDF. Use the edge that was even with the MDF as a starting point and trim all four sides. Next we will glue two oak pieces to the glue up design.

Cut four oak strips the thickness of the design. Make them whatever width you want. Cut the protruding ends off and glue strips of oak across the longer ends of the design. After the glue has dried, place the assembly upon the template and you will be able to determine what width the walnut boards will be required to complete the edges.

Photo 10-9: Glue the other two side edge oak pieces to the design

Photo 10-10: Place the assembly upon the template to see what size boards are required to complete the edges

Finish the lazy susan by following the same steps as shown in Chapter 9. That is, glue walnut to the edges, cut it out to a 16" diameter, route the edges, sand in progressive increments of sandpaper fineness, apply a 50/50 combination of linseed oil and paint thinner to bring out the grain. Complete with your favorite finish. Make a base as shown in Chapter 8 ("Creating a Base").

Photo 10-11: Finished Lazy Susan

11

Wood Laminated Design Projects
Cutting Boards, End Grain

There are basically two types of cutting boards. One being utilitarian and the other being decorative. The utilitarian one being where a person would use it for actually cutting and would have no qualms about putting a knife to it. The other being for decoration, would be much more expensive to purchase, be more labor intensive to create and therefore, would more likely than not, never have a have a knife used on it.

If you check on cutting boards online, you will find a variety of boards. Most are either made of end grain of expensive hardwoods or simple straight laminations of different colored hardwoods. In either case you will usually find that they are quite expensive. What we will do in this chapter is create attractive end grain boards using inexpensive yellow pine construction lumber and also beautiful cutting boards with very attractive designs.

We will start by creating a very easily made and inexpensive but quite attractive cutting board using end grain construction as shown in Chapter 7.

The EASY Way to Create End Grain Cutting Boards

Cut six pieces of end grain 1-1/4" thick, as shown in Chapter 7. The six pieces will be used to construct two different cutting boards.

Edge glue three of the pieces together. Since this comes out to 13" long, a standard 12" clamp will not work. If you do not have clamps longer than 12", simply cut 1/2" of each end so the clamps will reach. Using a damp rag, wipe off any glue squeeze out.

Photo 11-1: Edge gluing and clamping the three pieces

If you use Bessey clamps as shown, I recommend you use a sheet of wax paper under the boards to prevent glue build-up on the bar clamps.

After the glue has dried, the three pieces need to be sanded. Start with 60 grit sandpaper and remove all saw marks. Then sand with 80, 100, 120 and 180 sandpaper. Since we will be applying an oil finish it will not be necessary to go any finer than 180 on the sanding.

Photo 11-2:
Sanding the
board

Next, route the edges with a rounding over bit, preferably using a routing table. The size of the bit is optional and of your choice. End grain has a tendency to tear out and therefore you should make two or three gradual passes and not remove a lot at one time.

Photo 11-3:
Routing the
edges

After sanding the edges, a finish of mineral oil (not mineral spirits, that's a paint thinner) is applied. Cutting board finishes will be explained at the end of this chapter. The oil will highlight the grain and since this is yellow pine it will turn it yellow. It is best to apply several coats over a period of time.

Photo 11-4: Finished oiled board (still wet)

12

Wood Laminated Design Projects
Deluxe Cutting Board

By simply inserting other woods with the end grain, we can create a very attractive cutting board while still using the beauty and low cost of the end grain. Any contrasting wood may be used such as walnut or padauk. I chose to use padauk for this project.

Photo 12-1: End grain and paduak boards

I suggest you wipe the surface of the padauk with lacquer thinner or paint thinner to remove any oil. I would also advise you to wash off any padauk sawdust off of you soon after you are done as it can be toxic to your skin. Also be sure and wear a dust mask. The thickness of the board does not matter as it will be turned on edge. The padauk I had on hand is approximately 3/4" thick.

Cut four pieces of padauk or walnut 7-1/4" long and slightly wider than the thickness of the end grain. Cut two pieces 17" long the same width for the outside long edges.

Photo 12-2:
Alignment of pieces
with end grain

Glue the three pieces of padauk to the end grain pieces. The pieces should be slightly longer than the width of the end grain. These ends will be cut off flush in the next step.

Photo 12-3:
Gluing and
clamping the
boards together

After the boards have dried it will be necessary to cut the sides of the boards so they are even. This may be done on a radial arm saw as shown here or on a table saw.

Photo 12-4: Cutting the sides evenly

Glue and clamp the side pieces to the block. By placing wax paper below the boards, you will prevent the boards from sticking to the newspapers.

Photo 12-5: Gluing and clamping the side pieces

Using a radial arm saw or a table saw, cut off the end of the board to remove the protruding end pieces. Cut slightly into the end piece to ensure it being flush.

Photo 12-6: Cutting off the ends

The next steps will be of sanding and routing, the same as described in the last steps of the plain end grain cutting board, that is, after the glue has dried the three pieces need to be sanded. Start with 60 grit sandpaper and remove all saw marks. Then sand with 80, 100, 120 and 180 sandpaper. Since we will be applying an oil finish it will not be necessary to go any finer than 180. Then route the edges using a rounding over bit of your choice making two or three passes so as to not remove too much at one time. After routing, the edges will also need to be sanded smooth in preparation for the mineral oil finish.

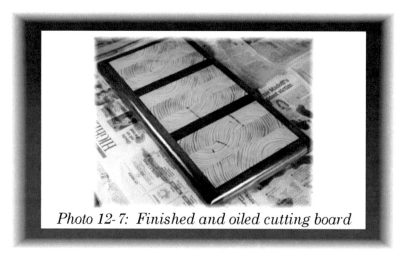

Photo 12-7: Finished and oiled cutting board

13

Wood Laminated Design Projects
Cutting Board, Wood Lamination Design

A quality wood cutting board offers several advantages over plastic. Cuts will normally "self-heal" on a wood board, wood has natural antiseptic properties to resist bacteria and mildew, and a cutting board made of wood is easy to resurface and less damaging to kitchen knives.

Make a wood design of your choice as shown in the *Techniques* Section on Wood Art Design. I will pick one from one of the designs already constructed.

I have picked this design made of walnut and maple. Either walnut or maple would be a good choice to use for the outside edges. We will use maple in this project.

Photo 13-1: Previously made wood design glue ups.

Photo 13-2: A walnut and maple lamination

This particular lamination runs at an angle on both ends and it is necessary to cut the corners off at a right angle to become square. Select a maple board approximately six inches wide and cut it down the middle. This will make the cutting board six inches wider and six inches longer than the glued up block. The board should be the length of the block plus seven inches. Since this block ended up being eight inches long , I cut the board to be 15" long.

Plane the maple board to be the same thickness as the laminated design block. Rip the board down the middle, giving you two boards, each 3 inches wide by 15 inches long. Rip one of these boards down the middle. Cut the other board in half. You should now have two boards that are 3 inches wide by 7-1/2 inches long, and two boards that are 1-1/2 inch wide by 15 inches long. Plane the *edges* smooth.

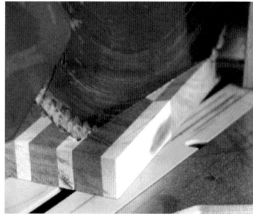

Photo 13-3: Cutting off the ends at a right angle

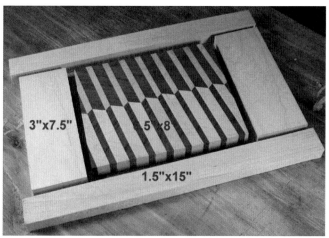

Photo 13-4: Lamination and maple edge pieces

Glue the edges of the two short maple pieces to the ends of the laminated board and clamp them. Notice the ends of these pieces protrude beyond the edge of the laminated board. This is to ensure a smooth finish when you trim the off the ends.

Photo 13-5: Gluing and clamping the short pieces to the glued up laminated board

Photo 13-6: Cut the sides of the glued up laminated board and the ends of the short pieces to be smooth

After the glue dries, cut off the protruding end pieces. Cut slightly into the lamination while doing this so that the edge of the cutting board will be smooth in preparation to gluing the longer side pieces on.

If you are using this type of clamp (Bessey), I have found that it is a good idea to put a piece of wax paper over the clamps, beneath the wood being glued. This prevents glue from getting on the bars which builds up and makes it difficult to adjust the clamps.

Glue the edge of each long piece to the edge of the laminated board, clamp, and allow the glue to dry. Then cut off the protruding ends of the long pieces to square up the ends.

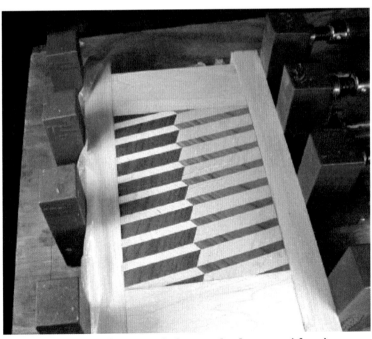

Photo 13-7: Glue and clamp the longer side pieces

Photo 13-8: Mark the ends using a board or measuring in from the edges

This next step is to cut a handle into the cutting board. *You may skip this step if you want* as it isn't really necessary but looks nice in cutting boards.

Working with one end of the cutting board only, make a mark 2" in from each side and cross the lines 2" in from the end. You may do this either by measuring with a ruler or using a board that is 2" wide. This will give you an "X" to locate the two drilling locations.

Center punch the two X's, and place masking tape on the board below the drill area to help prevent tear out. Place a board below the area to be drilled and use a 1-1/4" drill bit, preferably using a drill press if you have one with a Forstner type drill bit. Use a straight edge to draw lines between the outer edges of the holes. These will be the lines you will use to cut out the handle hole.

Photo 13-9: Drill out the two holes

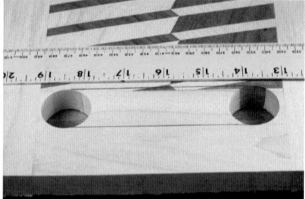
Photo 13-10: Using a straight edge draw a line between the outer edges of the holes

Using a jigsaw or scroll saw, follow the lines and cut out the handle hole. Then, using a rounding over bit of your choice of size with a router, route the edges on both sides and all outside edges. Maple is a very hard wood and tends to burn and also tear if you take too big a bite at one time. It is best to make a light pass at first and then gradually increase the depth of cut.

Photo 13-11: Follow the lines to cut out the handle hole

Photo 13-12: Route over the edges, top, bottom and outside edges of the board

Sand the board surfaces and edges starting with 60 grit sand paper and increasing to 180 grit. Give the board a thorough coat of mineral **oil** (*not* mineral spirits), available at a drug store or grocery store. After letting the oil soak in for about an hour, wipe it off using a paper towel or rag. Apply a couple more coats, letting dry for a day between coats.

Finishing

At one time there was a general concept in belief that wooden cutting boards trapped bacteria and that plastic cutting boards were preferable as they were safer. A University study proved just the opposite stating that a wood cutting board if properly washed would remove the bacteria, whereas a plastic board would still trap bacteria within the knife cuts and grooves in the plastic board. Cutting boards should periodically be sanitized. Never immerse the board in a sink full of water as the end grain

Photo 13-13: The cutting board after one coat of mineral oil

will soak up the water and can cause the board to crack. Instead, scrub the board periodically with soap and hot water. Vinegar is also a recommended sanitizing agent. Follow with another coat of mineral oil.

Never apply vegetable or cooking oils to a cutting board. The oil will eventually become rancid and give off a bad odor. Do not waste your money on so called Food Safe finishes.

I, along with many other cutting board makers prefer to apply four or five coats of mineral oil as mentioned above. Be sure it is **mineral oil** and *not* mineral spirits, as that is a paint thinner. Mineral oil may be reapplied periodically to keep it from drying out.

By applying beeswax and then buffing, it will not only enhance the appearance of the board by giving it more of a luster but it will also seal the wood and is perfectly food safe. I personally prefer to use it on the fancier laminated boards that will probably never have a knife taken to it. The other boards will also be enhanced initially by a beeswax application but it probably wouldn't be an ongoing thing with a board that is actually put to use as it is highly recommended that the boards be periodically cleaned and mineral oil be reapplied.

Photo 13-14: Completed cutting board, and another design using walnut edges

14

Wood Laminated Design Projects
Piggy Banks

The ever popular piggy bank has been around for a long, long time. Some have become popular collector's items. I have found that they make very nice baby gifts and gifts for young children.

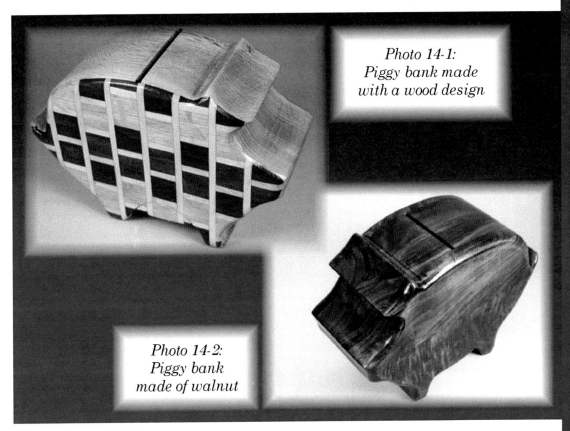

Photo 14-1:
Piggy bank made
with a wood design

Photo 14-2:
Piggy bank
made of walnut

In this chapter we will make a simple bank using veneering as shown in the *Techniques* section, however these banks can also be made using one of the glued up wood art designs or with solid lumber as shown in the photos above. All three use the same basic construction methods.

Photo 14-3:
Piggy bank pattern
(5.75" x 8.25" here, but
may be scanned or copied,
then enlarged as needed)

You may make piggy banks of pretty much any size. On the facing page, you see a pattern for a bank that (due to the size limits of the pages in this book) is 5.75" high and 8.25" long. However, you may scan or copy this page and pattern, then enlarge it as needed and print it out for your personal use.

I recommend that you use a rubber cement or paste stick to paste your printed copy of the pattern to a piece of thin paneling or thin MDF board. You may then cut it out on the band saw to use as a pattern to trace onto your actual project.

Photo 14-4: Picture of pattern pasted to paneling being cut out

Patterns for other animals are available from coloring books or online. The basic construction, however, remains the same. That is, an inside piece with the center cut out, two outside pieces glued on and then cut out following the pattern.

We will start this project by assuming that we have enlarged our pattern to make a bank that is 7" high by 11" long. We are using yellow pine for the center of the bank and 1/2" MDF board covered with a veneer, for the outside.

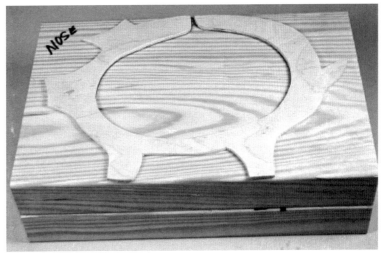

Photo 14-5: After gluing the two pieces together, place the pattern on the wood and mark the nose end on the block and the edge of the block

Using a standard piece of 2x8 construction lumber as shown in Chapter 7 of the *Techniques* section, cut two pieces 11" long and glue them together. Place the pattern on the wood block and mark the NOSE end on the block and top edge. Glue the top edges flush with each other. The bottom edges will be cut off.

Trace the center of the pattern onto the wood block. This is the only part that will be cut out of the center block at this time. Cut out the center, making sure that the "slot" is wide enough to accept coins but not too wide as to allow coins to be easily shaken out of the bank.

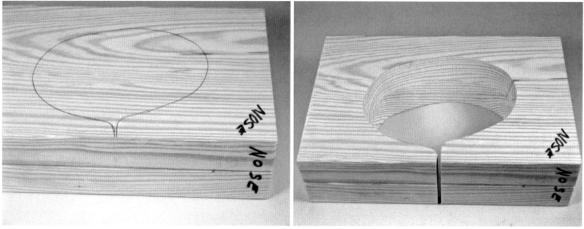

Photo 14-6: Trace the center of the pattern onto the block

Photo 14-7: Cut out the center

Select a piece of veneer to be used on the outsides. You may want to review the Chapter 6 tips on Veneering before proceeding here. Cut two pieces of 1/2" MDF board 7 1/2"x 11" to attach the veneer to. Spray water on both sides of the veneer to make it less brittle and much more easy to cut without tearing. Use a cutter with a new, sharp blade. Place the MDF upon the veneer and remove the excess veneer around the edges.

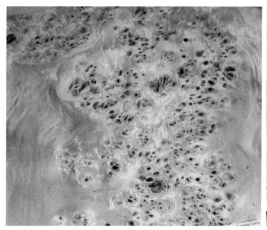

Photo 14-8: Select a piece of veneer to be used on the outsides of the bank

Photo 14-9: Use the MDF to cut off the excess veneer around the edges

So far what we have done could also be done with any solid wood such as walnut, oak, pine, maple, etc. The difference at this point is that instead of veneering a piece of veneer to a piece of MDF, you'd use a piece of 3/4" lumber or thinner for the outside pieces.

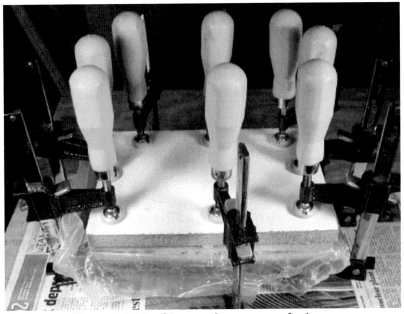

Glue the veneer to both pieces of the MDF boards. Place wax paper between the layers and make a sandwich of a piece of blank MDF, the two veneered pieces of MDF, an outside piece of blank MDF and clamp them together as shown in Chapter 6 – the difference being that you are veneering two pieces here rather than one. I often veneer six pieces at a time.

Photo 14-10: Clamp the veneered pieces together for the glue to dry

Clamp the two veneered outside sections to the inside block. Don't be concerned about excess glue runoff. It will all be removed when the pattern is cut out. However, you do not want glue to accumulate in the coin slot. Take a small piece of folded newspaper and remove any glue that may be there.

Photo 14-11: Clamp the two outside pieces to the inside block

Photo 14-12: Trace the pattern onto the block

*Photo 14-13: Follow the pattern
to cut out the bank*

Photo 14-14: Route the edges of the bank

After clamping and gluing the two outside veneered pieces to the inside block, place the pattern on the block with the nose of the pattern toward the NOSE end written on the block. Align the coin slot of the pattern with the slot cut into the block. Place the pattern slot at the top of the block. If the feet of the pattern are slightly too long, don't be concerned, they can be cut off slightly shorter.

Cut out the pattern on the bandsaw. I prefer to use a 3/16" blade with an aggressive 3 teeth per inch (TPI) blade. You may use a wider blade and also a finer tooth blade, if you want. A finer tooth blade will cut with less teeth marks but I prefer a more aggressive cut on something this thick. A more aggressive blade also works better with hardwoods. Remove the saw marks with 60 grit sand paper. Do NOT sand the veneer at this time. Veneer is very thin and should not be sanded with anything coarser that 220 sandpaper.

Use a rounding over bit with ball bearing guides to round over the edges of the bank. Move the bank from right to left against the router blade that is moving counter clock wise.

Place the pattern on the bank and make a pencil mark on the bottom of the pattern to mark where the bottom of the interior hole is within the bank. Place two pencil marks to mark the location of the legs. This will allow you to correctly align the cup in the next step.

Photo 14-15: Mark the bottom of the interior hole location

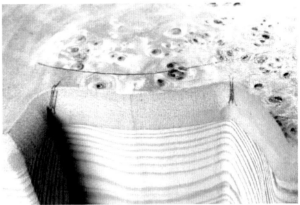

Photo 14-16: Mark the position of the legs

Using a paper cup or another round object of about 3" diameter, draw a line between the two marks made to indicate the position of the legs. This is to mark where you will be cutting a piece out of the bottom to be able to remove the coins. When I first made banks, I had a large cork in the bottom to remove the coins. Customers commented that it would be too easy for children to remove the money.

By looking at the two lines drawn, you can tell if the hole will be big enough. This "cup line" could be moved down as the "hole" does not have to be that large. The "cup line" is the line that will actually be cut. The other line is just to indicate where the bottom of the money hole is and how big a hole you will have. You will be sawing in from just inside the legs.

Photo 14-17: Mark the place to remove the bottom piece (plug)

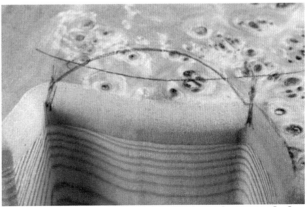

Photo 14-18: Check to see how large a hole will be made when the "plug" is removed

Make a pencil mark on both sides of the bank centered on the MDF pieces. Remember, everything between the MDF is a large cavity. Holes will be drilled in the MDF to allow removal and attachment of the "plug." Center punch these two marks to prepare for drilling and the countersinking of the holes.

A 1" drywall screw works well to secure the plug to the bottom of the bank. Using a 1/8" size grill bit, drill two holes into the MDF where you have previously marked and center punched the location. Drill over an inch deep to accommodate the screw. Use a countersink bit to allow the head of the screw so it will not be protruding above the surface of the bank. Do not put the screws in at this time.

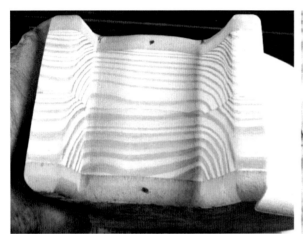

Photo 14-19: Mark the location of the holes to be drilled

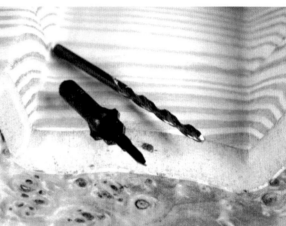

Photo 14-20: Drill and countersink two holes for the mounting screws

Using a band saw, carefully cut out the plug. After you have cut out the plug, you can see what a large hole is available to easily remove the money from the bank.

Photo 14-21: Cut out the plug using a band saw

Photo 14-22: The plug has now been cut out

Screw the plug back onto the bank. The plug is now secure and makes it more difficult for a young child to remove the money.

It is now time to further sand the bank. If you previously have removed the saw marks, you may now use 80, 120, 180 and then 220 grit sandpaper. It will probably be necessary to hand sand in certain areas where the orbital sander cannot reach. Again I must repeat, do NOT sand the veneer with anything coarser than 220 grit.

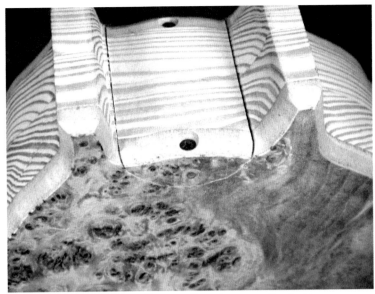

Photo 14-23: Screw the plug on the bottom and then finish the sanding process

After sanding apply a thin coat of 50/50 linseed and paint thinner. You may then apply your favorite finish, poly, lacquer, etc.

The Piglet Bank

This is an easy to make, inexpensive bank made entirely of end grain. Follow the previous instructions for making banks, only using a smaller pattern.

Photo 14-24: Small Piglet bank

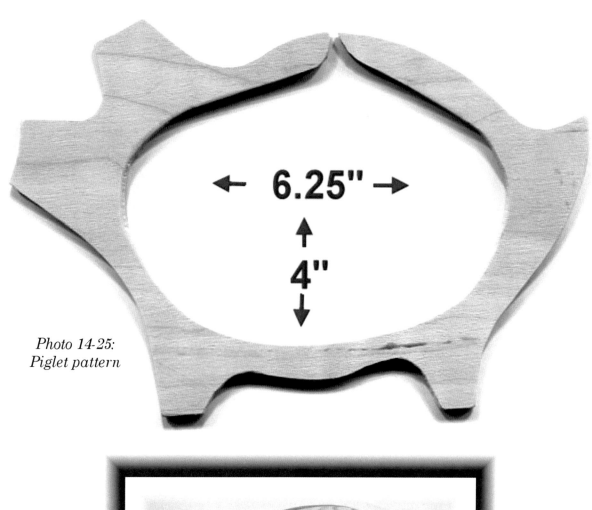

← 6.25" →

↑
4"
↓

Photo 14-25:
Piglet pattern

Photo 14-26: Finished Piggy Bank

15

Wood Laminated Design Projects
Pencil Boxes

We will be making a simple but attractive pencil box using end grain lumber as described in Chapter 7. We will start by using five of the 1/4" thick pieces that are 7"x4-1/4". Four of the pieces will be used to construct the sides and one piece for the bottom. We will be cutting the edges to 45 degree angle cuts. You could also glue the box together by simply butting the edges together which is easier and quicker but not quite as attractive.

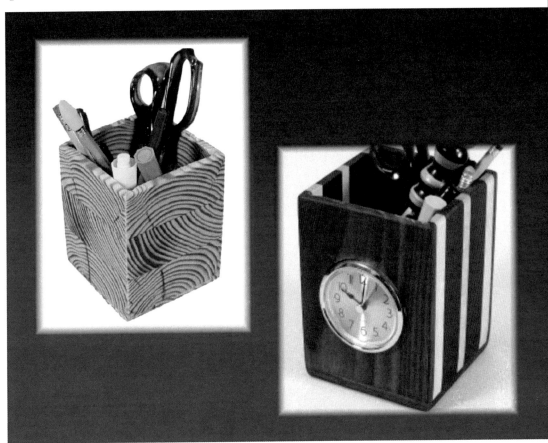

Start by sanding the pieces smooth on a belt sander if you have one. If not, then use a hand sander. I use 100 grit paper on the belt sander and 60 on the hand sander. The object here is to remove the coarse saw marks created when you saw end grain. The project will be fine sanded later after assembly. A piece that is only 1/4" thick can be difficult to hold on a belt sander.

I removed most of the deeper marks on the belt sander and then finished sanding with the orbital hand sander. I prefer to do my hand sanding upon a piece of scrap carpet. The carpet helps hold the piece in place and also prevents scratching on the bottom surface.

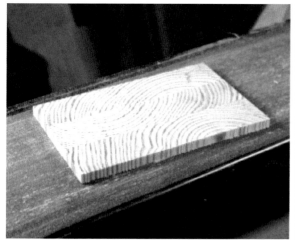

Photo 15-1: Sanding the pieces on a belt sander

Photo 15-2: Using a hand sander on the pieces

Using the miter saw, *cut one end off four* of the pieces at a 45 degree angle with the pieces held in a vertical position.

Photo 15-3: Cutting the ends at a 45 degree angle

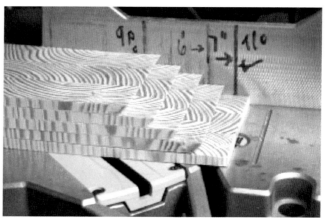

Photo 15-4: The four pieces plus the bottom after cutting <u>one</u> edge

Measure 4-1/2" from the beveled edge (long edge) and draw a mark. This will be the width of our pencil box. Flip the piece just marked so the beveled end is on the left with the mark on the right. Clamp a piece of scrap to the saw fence so that the mark will be under the saw blade.

Notice the direction of the angle on the left and the angle of the cut you will be making on the right. The saw has NOT been repositioned. Cut off this end of each piece at a 45 degree angle to produce the four sides of the pencil box as shown.

Photo 15-5: Cut the opposite ends at a 45 degree angle

Photo 15-6: The four sides and the base after cutting both edges of the sides

The next step is to glue the four sides together. The method I use is easy, accurate and fast to do. Lay the four side pieces with the beveled sides facing down. Place a straight board across the top to keep them in alignment. Place three strips of masking tape across them.

Turn the pieces over so the beveled cuts are facing up. Apply a bead of glue between the joints, including the end pieces. Use a glue brush to spread the glue.

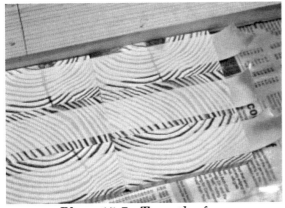

Photo 15-7: Tape the four pieces together

Photo 15-8: Spread the glue between the joints

Lift the pieces up and wrap them together. Using the loose tape at the ends, tighten the assembly into a box. Let dry and then sand the top and bottom so that the sides are even.

Photo 15-9: Wrap the tape around the box

Photo 15-10: Sand the top and bottom edges to make them flat and even

Take the piece that was selected for the bottom and place the box on top of it with two of the sides on the edges. Mark the other two sides with a pencil. Using the miter saw, cut the bottom piece to size.

Photo 15-11: Mark the bottom piece for size

Photo 15-12: Cut the bottom piece to fit the box

Put a bead of glue around the bottom edges of the box and clamp the bottom to the box. Place a board across the top of the box, so you will have a surface for the clamp to press against. Do not be concerned if the bottom does not fit perfectly as the bottom edge will be sanded evenly in the next step.

Photo 15-13: Clamp the bottom to the sides

After the bottom has dried, using 120 grit sand paper on the belt sander, sand the sides and rock the box forward so the bottom edges will be rounded off. Use a hand sander if you do not have a belt sander.

Finally, using a hand sander, sand all exterior surfaces starting with 120 then 180 and 220 grit sand paper.

Photo 15-14: Rounding off
the bottom edges

Photo 15-15: Finish sand the box
with 220 grit sand paper

Photo 15-16:
Bottom of
finished
box

Photo 15-17:
Box with
a clock
inserted

I have always preferred to wipe down or coat my finished products with an approximate 50/50 solution of linseed oil and paint thinner. If you use too much paint thinner it tends to soak into the wood and gives it an odor. If you use too much linseed oil it tends to dry sticky and shiny. I keep a used plastic coffee container filled with the mixture. By wiping a project with this solution it removes all saw dust, heightens the color and brings out the grain. End grain from yellow pine will not only bring out the grain but will also turn the wood orange. If you do not want your box to take on a pronounced orange color, skip this step and go on to your preferred finish. After the box has dried, at least overnight, you may then put on your favorite finish such as polyurethane, lacquer or just leave it with an oil finish.

Using the same methods only different materials, very attractive pencil boxes may easily be made. If you wish to insert a clock into the pencil boxes, find the center by drawing an X from corner to corner. Drill a hole in the center to fit the clock you are using. I prefer to drill the hole prior to assembling so that you can support the piece on the backside while drilling.

Photo 15-18: Draw an X on center to locate the hole for the clock

Photo 15-19: Various clock sizes

There is a large selection of clocks available from various woodworking and craft catalogs. There is quite a difference in prices for identical clocks depending upon where you purchase them so shop around.

Photo 15-20: Finished pencil box

16

Wood Laminated Design Projects
Making Boxes

T here are several books available on creating boxes. Many of these books contain the work of highly skilled and talented artists. Most of the boxes shown are true works of art requiring many, many hours of construction. The goal of this chapter is to show you an easy way to construct beautiful boxes using easy methods.

The box we will be building here uses a glued up walnut and oak checkerboard design as previously constructed in Chapter 3. *Photo 16-1* below shows this design, as well as the designs constructed in Chapter 5. You may construct and use any design you desire by following the guidelines in the *Techniques* section. The same basics also apply to making a box of solid lumber or of MDF board that has been veneered (see *Photo 16-2* below).

Photo 16-1: Pick a previously created design or make a new one

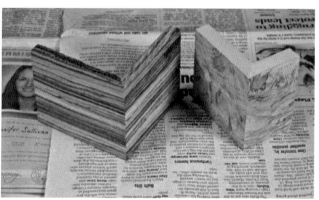

Photo 16-2: The box can also be made of solid lumber or a veneer

Using a walnut and oak checkerboard design, I resawed the pieces into 6.5" x 3-5/8" x 3/16" thick pieces. The thickness is not important as we will be gluing them to 1/4" MDF board. The length and height can also vary according to your own design. The construction methods will be the same. However, if you are using a checkerboard design as shown here, do not split any of the squares. Make sure you will have alternating square colors when the corners are assembled as shown in *Photo 16-4*. While I will be making a square box with all four sides the same length, if you want to make a long box rather than a square one, simply cut two of the pieces shorter. Be sure the walnut, oak pieces will align properly as shown in the photos below.

Photo 16-3: Select the design and size of the box you are making

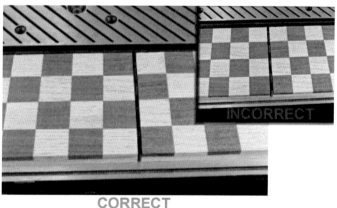

Photo 16-4: Correct alignment of wood colors

Using a piece of 1/4" MDF board, cut a strip longer than the sum of the design pieces laid end to end with approximately a 1/2" gap between. In this case, it came out to about 28".

Glue the four pieces to the MDF board. Here I glued one edge using an abundance of clamps. On the other edge, I used less clamps by placing a board across the edge, distributing the clamping pressure and therefore requiring fewer clamps. Be sure and glue one edge even with the edge of the MDF board.

Photo 16-5: Design pieces laid out on 1/4" MDF board in preparation for gluing

Photo 16-6: Gluing and clamping the pieces to the MDF board

Photo 16-7: Sand the pieces while still glued to the long piece of MDF

After drying, this is a good time to sand the saw marks out using 60 grit sandpaper while still glued to the MDF board. This will give you a larger piece to hang onto while sanding. Separate the four pieces by cutting them apart. You will now have the four sides with edges that need to be trimmed off.

Photo 16-8: Cut the pieces apart from each other

Photo 16-9: The four sides of the box with MDF that needs to be removed

When you glued the design pieces to the MDF, you were told to glue one edge even with the edge of the MDF board. Take each of these pieces and sand them to remove any glue and to ensure that they are perfectly flush and square with the sides.

The next step is to remove all of the MDF from the edges. Start by placing the edge that you just sanded flush against the fence so that your cuts will be square.

Photo 16-10: Sand the bottom edge of the side pieces to be flush and square

Photo 16-11: Remove all MDF showing on the edges

With all four side pieces aligned properly with alternating walnut/oak squares, mark a "B" on the inside bottom edge of each piece. This is so you will cut the groove to hold the bottom of the box on the correct edge.

We will now cut a slot into the bottom edges of the sides that we had previously marked with a "B" to accommodate the box bottom. I will be using 1/4" MDF board which works very well for box bottoms. Use a 1/4" veining router bit and set your fence to cut the groove 1/4" from the bottom of the box. Set the depth so it will be cutting about half way into the MDF board which will be about 1/8". All boards are not necessarily the same thickness.

Photo 16-12: Mark a "B" on the bottom edge of each piece, alternating wood colors together

Photo 16-13: Cutting the groove for the box bottom

The bottom should fit loose but not sloppy. If it is too tight you may have to readjust the fence slightly and make the groove a little wider. If it fits tight you will not be allowing room for expansion with temperature and humidity changes.

Each of the four side pieces need to have the corners cut at a 45 degree angle. This can be easily done using the miter saw. Do not take off any more than is necessary but you should have a "sharp edge" after cutting.

All four side pieces should now have their corners cut at a 45 degree angle. With the outside surface facing up, align the pieces so that the walnut and oak pieces will be alternating, and with the bottom edges against a strip of wood, apply three pieces of masking tape across the assembly to tie them together.

Photo 16-14: Four pieces with
45 degree angles cut on both ends

Photo 16-15: Align the pieces, then
tape them together with masking tape

Flip the assembly over and double check that all of the grooves for the box bottom are aligned with each other. Wrap the box together and secure the end with tape. This is temporary. Place the box upon a piece of paper with the corner edge inside of the box. Mark the other inside edges with a pencil. This will give you an exact measurement of the box which can be used later during lid construction.

Photo 16-16: Checking to see that
the grooves for the bottom are aligned

Photo 16-17: Mark the size of
the box upon a piece of paper

You may now cut out the pattern you have made and by making the box bottom piece using 1/4" MDF board slightly larger than the pattern you will have a piece that will fit nicely. Do not make the piece to fit too tight, better to allow room for expansion. By loosening the tape at the end of the box, you can open it up to check the bottom for fit after you cut it.

Photo 16-18: Use this pattern to cut out the box bottom and/or top

A second method of cutting a bottom to size is by leaving everything taped together, open up one end. Place the bottom piece within the grooves cut for the bottom. You may use 1/4" MDF board or a scrap piece of paneling that you may have lying around. Mark the edges where it would fall slightly inside of the adjoining grooves in the other two side pieces. Cut the bottom at these marks, insert it into the grooves, and wrap the sides around the bottom to check for fit. You should not have glued anything at this time.

Photo 16-19: Mark the edges of the bottom piece

Photo 16-20: Insert the bottom and check for fit

Open the box up at one edge while still taped together. Apply glue to the edges and spread evenly with a glue brush. After gluing, close up the box after inserting the bottom. Tape the ends shut. If you have rubber bands that will fit, it doesn't hurt to add a few for extra clamping power but it is not necessary.

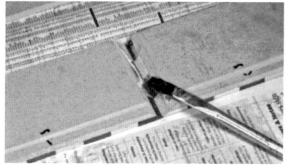

Photo 16-21: Apply glue to the edges

Photo 16-22: Insert bottom and tape shut

Now that the basic box is complete, two things remain to be done: lining the box (which is optional) and making a lid or top for the box.

Photo 16-23: Completion of basic box without a lid

Lining the Box

For several years I have lined my boxes with felt. Today there is a craft foam less than about 1/8" thick available in a large range of colors. It is inexpensive, easy to work with and available at most craft stores in the same section as felt.

Place the felt/foam piece upon the box and mark the corners so that you can cut a piece to fit the bottom. They both cut easily with scissors but if you happen to have a paper cutter it is even better. Cut the piece to size and glue it to the bottom using your carpenters wood glue and a glue brush.

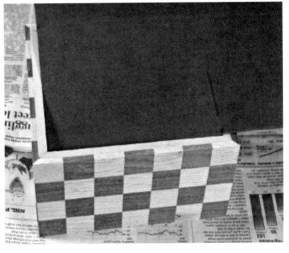

Photo 16-24: Cut the liner to fit the bottom of the box

If you are using the foam as shown here, cut each side individually and glue to the sides. If you are using felt, you can use longer pieces and they will wrap around the inside corners more readily than the foam.

Photo 16-25: Line the inside of the box

Making a Lid

There are several ways to make simple, attractive lids without going through the hassle of attaching hinges. However on a box any larger than this one, you may prefer to use hinges.

Cut a piece of walnut or oak so it is 1/2" longer and wider than the box. This will give you 1/4" overlap on each of the four sides. Using the router, bevel the four edges. I used a cove bit here but a Roman Ogee bit works well also – but you may use whatever pleases you.

The cove bit I use is 1.5" diameter but a smaller bit could be used. Do not make the cut in one pass. Make your cuts gradual by raising the bit in steps.

I made a second cut on the edge of the first cut by moving the fence rearward and by lowering the cove bit. The second cut isn't necessary, I am just showing another option in the cutting of the edges. Again make the cuts gradual by raising the bit in steps. After making the final pass, leave the router bit setup to be used again for the second cut on the top as shown in *Photo 16-29*.

Photo 16-26: Cut the top out of either walnut or oak

Photo 16-27: Route the four edges of the top

Photo 16-28: Using a cove bit on the four edges

Photo 16-29: Making a second cut on the edges of the top

Since this a "How To" book, I will take the box top design one step further. You may not wish to use this step but go with the solid walnut or oak top which is very attractive. Using some of the checkerboard design that was created earlier, I will resaw a piece to about 1/8" thick.

Photo 16-30: Resawing a piece to be used in the box top

Cut the piece that you just created by resawing the design glue up so that it is the same size as the raised portion of the top. *Be careful to equalize your cuts so that you do not have a full block showing on one edge and only half of a block on the opposite side.* Glue it to the top.

Make the cut again, using the same setup of the bit that you previously made in *Photo 16-28*. This will cut an edge on the piece you just glued to the top.

Photo 16-31: Gluing the resawn design piece to the box top

Photo 16-32: Cutting an edge on the piece just glued on

Now that we have created a top for the box, the next step is to create a way to hold the top to the box itself. I have three different methods for doing this without using hinges. For any of these methods, the initial step is to cut a pattern the size of the inside of the box. If you did this when making the box bottom (*Photo 16-18*), double check to ensure that it is indeed the size of the interior of the box. Center it on the inside of the box top and tape it to the top. Using a pencil, mark the four corners.

Photo 16-33: Taping the pattern to the inside of the box top

Method 1 - Drill two holes in opposite corners inside of the corners marked on the lid and insert dowels. Be careful when drilling, not to drill completely through the lid. That would be a disaster at this point. (Note: The photo shown, *Photo 16-34*, is of a lid for a different sized box than the one we were making.)

Photo 16-34: Using dowels to hold the top in place

Method 2 - Cut two strips of wood, slightly shorter than the corners previously marked on the top. Glue them to the top, INSIDE of the corners previously marked. (See *Photo 16-35*.)

Photo 16-35: Using strips of wood to hold the top in place

Method 3 - Cut a piece of 1/4" MDF board approximately 1/8" smaller than the opening, allowing for the box lining if you installed one, Check to see if it will fit in the opening, prior to gluing it to the top. Don't make it too tight if you have previously lined the box. Center it on the lid while gluing to the top. (See *Photo 16-36*.) Note: This is the method I used for the box built during this project and shown on the completed box in *Photo 16-37*.

Photo 16-36: Centering and gluing a piece to the inside of the top

Photo 16-37: The completed box

Now that you know the basics of box making, let your imagination run wild and create simple and elaborate boxes. I will show you a few other boxes I have made.

Photo 16-38: Wedding box

The beautiful box in *Photo 16-38* was created by purchasing an inexpensive box with a curving lid from a large chain craft supply store. I then covered the sides with veneer and added wavy cut pieces from maple and zebrawood, although any wood may be used. It comes with the hinges already attached which is another plus. I lined the box but of course that is optional. This is a quick and easy way to create attractive boxes as they are available in various sizes and shapes.

Sometimes as a woodworker you decide to let your imagination run wild and create something unusual just for yourself and your own satisfaction.

Such is the case in the piece below in *Photo 16-39*. It consists of three boxes that were turned on a lathe and then stacked upon each other. It consists of various hardwoods with the predominate one being zebrawood as used in the top pieces and the bottom supporting pedestal. The whole assembly is 21" tall and resides in a showcase in my home.

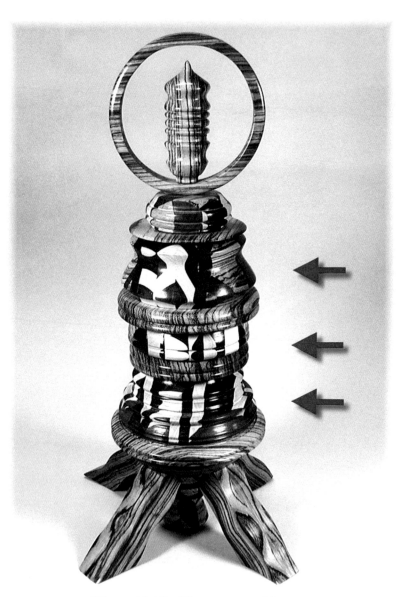

Photo 16-39: Three turned boxes

Made in the USA
Las Vegas, NV
17 December 2023

83023429R00059